The Silence Of A Butterfly

Poems of Indifference

Tapas Chatterjee

Dedication

To Thea, my six-month-old daughter, a bundle of
mischief and happiness;
and Suparna, my rock-solid support and better half.

Preface

Emptiness and unfulfillment in love weave a haunting theme in poetry, capturing the ache of longing and the void left by unreciprocated emotions. It speaks of silent nights where whispered hopes dissolve into echoes, of hands once held now grasping only air. Love, once radiant, fades into a hollow space where memories linger like ghosts, beautiful yet unreachable. The heart, heavy with unsaid words and unanswered dreams, searches for solace in verses that mirror its sorrow. In this emptiness, poetry finds its power—transforming loss into lyrical beauty, painting absence with the ink of yearning and unfulfilled desires.

Acknowledgements

Heartfelt gratitude to all who read and truly understand
the poems—their depth, their beauty. And also to those
who may not engage with the words but still appreciate
the effort. A simple, 'Good stuff, Tapas! Keep writing.
Why not publish your work?' means the world.
Believe me, appreciation in any form is always welcome
and deeply valued!😊

1. If I write an ode tonight...

A thousand desires, sweet and salt
melt over my eyebrows and tongue.
Slowly and steadily skin burns and tans.
The ocean filled in a balloon glass
breaks the giant concretes on the shore
and pulls me back to you.
If I write an ode tonight, it has to be you.
If I hum a love ballad, can someone listens to it?
The whistling branches of Gulmohar beside my open
window
washed in the moonlight bow down humbly, head
lowered.
The buried old, crumpled love letters
still heave and breathe in a mysterious hope in a forlorn
place.
The rhythms of the heartbeats
and rhymes of the word woven meticulously
culminates in you, in perfect ecstasy and a quiet melody.

2. I get drawn to you...

I get drawn to you..
a bit mindless and in a slight
conscious spree,
like a breathing firefly, a pulling magnet,
a disobedient bumble bee.
More of a suffering fever, a venomous serpent,
a fast jungle fire, it spreads over me
from head to toe and eyes to mind, mind to heart
in an outlandish jiffy.
Everything stays; an abeyance; a stalled journey.
No differentiation of wrong from right,
O yes, you are certainly not a fairy
with wings exquisite,
Nor do you get those dimples
when you smile blithely.
Eyes are quite simple and lone,
Certainly, lips could have been poutier and a little bold.
Heard a lot about the marks on the moon,
that has increased the urge to manifold,
obvious from the stories of Chakor's croon.

Why does the thirsty earth
long for the monsoon bursts,
an adventurous moth
has a desire to get burnt,
the night wants to melt
into a fading dawn?

3. Lady of the night

You are no more what you used to be,
I doubt you accept it as true.... but I know it precisely.
Maybe you don't have anyone who tells you this
or loves you the way I would.
You still bloom O' Lady of the Night,
gorgeous and aromatic but lone, insensitive, and
ignorant.
Your elegance is still preserved in the stillness of my eyes
like the fragile dew pearls fallen over the velvety spread
of grass all over.
The silence in your eyes, the slumbering beauty still
seeps out of you
and touches my eyes, skin, veins, and entire body.

4. You have to come.

If you don't come, the night will wane in darkness
You know, this moon, these stars would be overlooked
forever.
The roses will droop one by one in the eerie silence of
the night's garden
and what remain will be thorns and prickles between
you and me
and this glittering in my eyes meant for you would fade
forever.
My darling, it's okay if you come at least concealing lies
in your eyes,
fire in your breath and knife and dragger in your hands.
I would welcome you.
Come if you can, even if you smear poison on your hair,
lips, neck and forehead
and more venom on your hands and body.
I promise I will kiss you like ever.
You break, shatter or get detached,
but you can always come to me

like the rivers meander all across
and finally meets the ocean.

6

5. You have become a moon

You have become a white moon for me;
no exchange of words,
no barter of emotions.
Entire night hours I look at you
and you look at me
(or may not be)

If I tell you something,
you will not understand.
You will give a damn or simply a deaf ear
or you fidget with your colourful bangles
and those dangling earrings.
I know, you will lower your eyes
and simply pretend not to know even a bit of it.
The clock will tick-tock and time takes wing
Clocks are mercilessly right;
Time eats everything, distorts everything,
but never quenches the thirst,
never answers the questions.
Questions that I had to ask you,

Questions that you were answerable to.
(or may not be)

Do you expect me to keep speaking to
the moon, the stars, the trees, and the rivers?
Their eternal silence despises me now.
Silence is sometimes mundane and boring.

Would leaving everything behind be an apt answer
It will not be a solace to the erupting volcanoes of the
heart
The question would remain unanswered
to whoever survives last
(or may not be)

6. The glint in those eyes is not to be forever....

When I look at you, I know
the glint in those eyes is not to be forever
at least not for me, I guess so.
The laughs, the giggles, the chuckles might have a shelf
life,
Have you not seen the waning moon or the ebbing tides?
The unending tender stories between us can cease one
day
to be replaced by an exchange of bland smiles
beyond our realization and outside our understanding.

If it rains now, would prefer not to be a bystander
anymore,
merely to watch it from the windows of my heart.
Who knows when the monsoon will break again
and if at all the clouds loom again,
whether it would be just for me, or not.
Expectations are rivers that die out
before becoming a part of the ocean.

Have you ever seen the raindrops that sit together side
by side
on the window rails and tend to get closer to each other,
or like the wanton free-floating wooden log
comes nearer to the riverbank
or simply the moon to the earth.
You may consider, we were one of them.
The parched birds that drank water from the same river
The streams of water that had a journey together
before the eternal separation.
Eyes might well up, smarting with tears
but time heals everything, isn't it?
Pangs will drown the heart and mind
but time heals everything, you know this.

7. Your Indifference

If you could touch my body
and feel the stillness of my night,
the difficult silence between us,
the trapped fragrance of tube-rose
kept inside my closed poetry book
over my unfinished poem,
the climbers would grow in my heart
to reach up to the mouth
and be flowered over my tongue.
If my feelings do not knock at your heart,
our paths would also not cross each other for sure.
I would not look at that moon or tuberoses anymore.
The days am spending disregarded,
shall make my final hours more potent
than my willingness to live.
That day would not be far when
I have to spread my hands
for every thread of breath inhaled and exhaled.
When I die, dare you to cry for me
as that was my part of destiny

and shall end with my last journey,
you are fated to be happy
like the raindrops that get separated from the cloud
rush to meet the thirsty land,
like the newfound freedom of some caged birds
not willing to touch the ground.
Listen, would you keep my final request?
you lock your lips to my lips
before they place my body on the pyre,
before the fire eats my body part by part,
before the love in my heart and eyes get charred to ash.
That day I know you will taste the sweetness
of the fruits dangling on the climbers
grown in my heart and ripened on my tongue.

8. Sit beside me

Put your hand on your heart and tell me candidly,
don't you look for to being seated beside me for hours,
like the moon that sits at the cusp of the tall tree
nonchalantly,
or the rain-fed clouds that lower themselves to touch the
thirsty earth passionately
Am no more able to maintain a pace with the wheels of
time,
that runs faster than the beats of my heart and its
emotions.
The morning travellers have called me by my first name
several times
before they resumed their journey, a bit nervous and
baffled.
My bleak zeal and excitement are insufficient to keep me
breathing
for how many more closed and unwelcoming doors of
the hearts
shall I knock for a desire of overwhelming sumptuous
alms?

Now, if you place your touch on my heart, it shall pacify me and make me calm.

14

9. My Sparrows and Bulbuls

Now the cups of elixir shall ask me
where I was these days.
Didn't I long for the tavern, the house of deprived,
and will nag to touch my lips
and force herself on me
like that mischievous penurious mistress
crafty enough to seduce as per her wish.
But I would not touch her
No, certainly I would not touch her.
I am happy and content, my missing lover,
my sparrows and bulbuls
have resumed appearing
in my garden of memories again.

10. You,Yes Only You!

You are a stream of a river
that comes closer and then goes far
If I get the moment to talk to you
I can barely look at the twinkles of your eyes,
the curves of your pouty lips
the prominence of the dimples in your cheeks.
Settle down for some moments, please
like a placid stillness of pond water,
like a complete lull before the mighty storms.
Give me a chance to fill my eyes with you, yes only you!
Let me speak out, let me laugh, let me crack those silly
jokes
Let me be what I used to be
A naked unalloyed pristine soul
But only in front of you, yes only you!

11. If I write to you

I can't simply think through my fingers
when I write to you.
My thought plucks the fresh flowers,
Drenches in the rain,
Rides the white horses of the advancing tides,
Sways like a dingy boat
against the streams of river Hooghly,
Shakes like the old village bridge when the train passes
while its whistle hangs on the silence of the night,
Dances in madness and pure joy, the verdant trees
when the gusty storm passes through its branches,
Participates in the evening cacophony of retreating birds
on the treetop during sundown,
Buzzes over the juicy blooming flowers for its nectar,
When a baby babbles and entwines her fingers
with that of her mother for her undivided attention,
When the end of the day, during the dusty sunset
herd of cattle retreat to their sheds,
When it orbits the sun and travels to the moon and stars.
...... And then, you know I could write those enchanting

words for you,
pure and pristine like the colours of the rainbow.

18

12. A mere sustenance...

I have seen the alluring bends of heaven on earth.
A sumptuous life, a wineglass filled to the brim,
if spills it is intoxication, if holds a charm.
Joys, beauty, abundance like a manna from skies wide
open.
A snail-like hope that neither moves nor dies,
a conch snail that makes smooth, shiny pearls of life.
A life that wakes up daily and goes out
to enter the world's cobweb for sustenance
and comes home to die again,
keeping the hope of night lantern alight.

13. Did you say that

Did you say that,
or I heard it on my own, don't know
maybe your voice hangs
on the silence of night's sorrow
or falls like a dead flower
that droops in absolute silence.
The whispers of mango orchard
have an inimitable sweetness
of Koyel's cuckoo
and its moving intoxicating madness.
Could have written something for sure
on the pristine white body of that moon
holding your ring finger in my hand
like some ancient stylus.
I wonder if I could even write a fraction
of what I want to write on the moon.
My emotions are indomitable and never-ending
and the surface wanes interval days of every fifteen.

14. Can't write anymore

Those days I would write abundant rhymes and paeans
from nocturnal moon hours
to setting sun
than what I could write for you today in an open letter
sitting in this deserted tavern.
You are aware, I had written poems on your eyebrows,
captured the experiences of life and its throes,
like a portraitist painted the auguries of passing seasons
But see the conspiracy of my will against my
determination
the words don't play in my mind anymore
nor I get that wisdom,
My fingers feel no more
the dance of my mighty pen.
Thoughts play the notorious game
of hide and seek like a mischievous Sun
and disappears in the lap of the dark mists,
day after day, not to say
being out of sight besides out of my mind,
leaving my heart's sky shadowed

by your long cobweb
of lush black hair hovering over.
Though sometimes I get to read
my thoughts
when the sun comes downhill
to take a dip in that nearby creek,
when the inside of my mind,
I get intermittent appearances of your silhouette
like I am swinging between life and bereavement.

15. Kiss

When you come near me
between my stretched arms,
the fragrance of your body will melt over me
against my bare chest; its warmth.
You carry with you a half-broken moon,
and keep the faith; I will surely surrender my world to
you.
One small touch of my lips
shall open the petals of your mouth
that store the honey of sweetest beehives.
Ah, let me kiss and suck this divine sweetness for many
more hours.
In the dark, the fire of our strongest desires could
twinkle like fireflies,
but our deep secrets would get mantled with no traces of
smoke to fly.
Let me rub my lips on your lips, to convey my feelings
like a rhymester writes his ballad
over a piece of paper with his chosen ink.
If you desire you can nibble and smear mine

with your pairs of rose petals
hued in bold red or of the colour of a matured wine.
If I kiss you now, am afraid that all night-blooming
Jasmines
shall shed and cover the ground out of acute shyness,
If I hug you tighter, I will not be baffled
to see the clouds start pouring on this darkest night.
And what if it happens to me that in my spell
I touch you deeper and feel you everywhere,
you will surely retract yourself like a 'touch me not'.
Beyond this carnal pleasure,
there is a world
where we will walk together
towards that milky white moon
our fingers entwined
where our souls would be one
and bodies closer.

16. I want to be a river

You want me to be like an ocean
that possesses a heart big enough
to allow the myriad rivers of emotions
to add the brine and filth
collected from every nook and corner.
You expect me to be level-headed and calm
like that deep serene ocean
that never swells with anger and pride,
and seldom trespasses the limits.
But I don't mind being a tempestuous
and indomitable river sometimes,
that surges in rain,
arrogant and incapable of concealing emotions.
One that roars like a rebel
and destroys what comes in its path,
not to be abided by any periphery,
rules and regulations.
It expresses what it hauls within
before settling down once more
as a nonchalantly flowing rejuvenated river.

17. Unanswered love

If you see a garland withered in the hope of getting
offered to that divine stone
If the lamp that was lit in front of my almighty flickers
gets scared in lone
If the myriad colours of flowers ready to be ornamented
get stampeded
If the sand castles of hope and determination of that
hapless juvenile are ruined
He is that insane, whose eyes get blurred waiting for the
clouds to burst over ever-thirsty land

18. Hide and seek

Who cares whether rains have ever descended there
again
The pregnant clouds might have refrained from crawling
down
Easterlies have stopped bringing with them the flock of
birds
Showers of heavy rains no more lashes about the face
The slap of winds might have levelled our built
sandcastles
I doubt if flowers have ever bloomed in gardens in the
last few years
For me, death enveloped everything the day you played
the final hide-and-seek
Now you are hiding your face in indefinite darkness and
don't know what I will seek.

19. My playmate

Who stalled my play when the end was yet to be
acknowledged,
My toys got scattered and my mate suddenly called it a
day.
The home that I started to build around my heart had to
be destroyed
Like in a heavy tremor, a pot of hope gets destroyed into
shards of clay.
Shall I wait to meet you my friend again or it will be a
desire in vain,
My return to where I had started will take time and it is
about to rain.
Pangs of heart have no language or They would have
surely conveyed to you,
If I get to arrange my play again someday, like a miracle
hope I'll see you.

20. If you stop liking me..

If you stop liking me,
if you choose not to talk to me the way you used to,
I can't do much but can only wait
like an empty boat waiting on the shore of a river,
and a torrid, charred earth looks at the clouds for hours.
How a bird unable to return timely to its nest
gets drenched in the rain; waits for the downpour to
stop.
And a newborn tries to convey his hunger to one and all.

Certainly I will knock at the doors of your heart
once... twice and maybe some more times
and would pass by like an Easterly,
a rain-fed wind of a strong monsoon
or a fleet of Siberian migratory birds
never to come back soon.

Even if you cease to exchange words, I can't request you
anymore
and can only wait to hear the soothing voice of yours.

Don't know, I may not feel the warmth and oneness,
and the distance of an arm length can alter
to a lightyear gap between our hearts.
You shall be surrounded by your friends, foes,
admirers, adversaries...laughs and cries
and varied colours and hues
but only seldom will I come to you
to bother you and be with you again....

21. Aloof

You remind me of some unmarked graves
I happened to see somewhere in the burial place,
where no one lights the candles; no one prays.
Algae, weeds, wild grasses and fallen leaves
maketh a shroud for ages.
No one plugs the agape ratholes beneath the Headstone.
Termites and ants make their colony,
Spiders, mites, ticks, and scorpions
breed and multiply merrily.

Maybe you wanted to be indifferent
to the tall talks, fake emotions,
cries and cacophonies of the world;
the random false care and consolations,
One sleeps in the backyard of the church, grand
yet away from God and distant to all around.

22. It rains in your eyes

It rains in your eyes
and drizzles in my mind.
If you open the soaking lids
even once of your eyes,
the floodgates would open
inside the silence of my mind.
Everything would wash away
along the profound earth's sway.
Nothing would remain the same
today, tomorrow, and what is endless.
I do understand your heart wrenches,
eyes cry without a yell,
as it makes its path from your soulful eyes
to my accepting heart's well,
after meandering the long, forlorn paths
of my dampened mind's dwell.

Allow me to empty into my eyes,
what you hold in those pair of sad eyes,
or let me sip the drops of agony and aches,

of your beautiful, moist eyes,
like one drinks the priciest of the spirits
and gets high.

Hold my hand, and let's walk some path,
the pain would ebb, and so would stop the rains.
The brightest of the stars
would dangle again,
from the highest of the heavens.

23. Neither yours nor mine

This happiness and sorrow
are neither yours nor mine.
Have thought of it several times,
if I could have placed my head
on your bosom and cried,
my grief would have ceased,
no more to be a resonance of just mine.
They tell me ill about you
and I pay heed to it half-heartedly
as it is reasonable to confront
their dishonest intention
with my small pretention.
I know, the moon looks what it looks
because of those black scars only.

24. Now comes the night

Now will come the pain,
Now the whirlwind would
toss the heaps of old dead fallen leaves,
Now the heart would bleed,
Now the heaviness of emotions
would weigh down the oceans of my heart,
Now I would sink into silence,
Now comes the night.

25. Black

The olden days swiftly loom
like the monsoon clouds,
so adamant; neither it disperses nor it pours.
Humid and suffocates
like the mighty gush of lungful east wind
that carts pain, heartbreak, loss, and death;
the death of someone dear.
Sometimes, I feel what I do is a mere repetition of
what I did yesterday or the day before.
Heart afraid of swapping thoughts with strangers.
I choke my neck with my own quivering hands
to abate the strong intermittent anguish and pain.
I can't anymore shield the light from the forces of dark
I shiver at the thought of
even a single lapse from my end;
If all happens, it will be completely dark
like the unknown expanse of the blackest skies
of a starless night, a creepy dead night.
Lord! I am afraid of the night;
I am so scared of the absence of light.

26. An imperfect painting

Feathers of a dove ..... O my tender love
promised to fly in a flock as seasonal birds
miles and miles in the open sky.
The icy breeze, the drizzling rains,
the scent of part evergreen Mahogany
all are there as innocent as thee.
The drenched woods, the blackest clouds hovering above,
desperate to kiss the top of trees,
the water-soaked earth, wildflowers, lotus and water
lilies
nothing could be more picturesque.
Alas....
Flawless not, the strokes of a paintbrush.
Colour fades as fondness wanes
in mate's heart,
respect diminishes as a tear rolls down
like colour drips over an open canvas,
colours convincingly mixed to create hues
and self-identity disappears.

27. Summer inside my heart

My angst and the scorching Sun
both simmer simultaneously
day after day like the cruel months of midsummer
as the chunks of lignite burn slowly
inside a furnace, red and purple.
What fuels the round auburn beast, I don't know
but my heart pumps the red kerosene
of suffered betrayal, mistrust and inability to my body.
Pains, it burns when the red venom spreads across the
veins slowly, little by little.
The cover of rain clouds, its intermittent showers
offer some relief from the outer temperature.
Sometimes, the heart soaked in tears
that welled up in my pair of eyes
allow me to remain calm and unaffected inside.

28. Opinion and Woman

Opinions about me are many, as there are many wagging
tongues,
they lick their own beliefs and store it in the stomach,
and many puke it at every turn.
It's amazing to see tall trees bending themselves during a
heavy storm,
Undoubtedly aware I am, pens that praise in public can
stab if confronted alone
But their hands never get tired of writing poetry on my
eyebrows
But beauty should have its freedom,
liberty is not yours to pluck the flowers
and to crush them in tedium.
Don't elevate me to a stature of God,
I am happy even if you treat me as an equal match to
every simple Man
I am most afraid of the conduct of those who never
respect God.

29. Adam and Eve

Dear Eve,

Didn't we have bites of apple from the same forbidden
tree?
We played the same silly games at Eden in our childhood
spree.
You always had a liking for weaving emotions of vibrant
colours
that my heart was unable to comprehend more than a
mere follower.
Remember I, you held to your bosom the lifeless babies
of some unknown breeds,
that day, ordinary was the blue sky's pouring
but mystifying and unfamiliar was your blue eyes'
shedding tears.
Perhaps your mildness I had taken as fearfulness.
I got to realize your character the day you saved me from
that hungry animal's jaws,
I was baffled to see how you had added your love,
sacrifice, compassion
and a tint of smile that you bore for me to complete my

life.
Undeniably we have limited time to live in this garden
but unlimited life to live.
Forever Your's Adam

30. My birthday wishes

You wished me my years bounty with the heavens, but
why?
Waited so many years for my evening sky
to speak to me
and today what happened,
you burnt my green jungles,
blew hurricane in my heart.
I have to recount the ages
that were elongated in your hurrying hand.
Would you listen to a tale of a river
that never met the ocean;
huh, you give a damn.
You know, when you left,
they consoled me showing the thorns grown
on your tongue and body.
Who would convey to them
that I had craved those red roses only?
You held the hand that was stronger and stout,
indeed you were as practical as you are today.

Long ago I had lost the heaven
and abhorred this very rational world.

43

31. Before I leave

My existence here can culminate any day
I shall pack my sack and move to a place unknown.
Prefer not to carry any belongings, don't know till when
and where I have to travel.
That day, if the corner of your eyes well up with tears,
don't cry.
If your heart searches me in every face you ought to see,
I beg you don't cry.
No need to run behind me to hand over my belongings
that I could miss to carry along,
If possible hand over my earnings that I deserve before I
leave forever.
Bestow me with some reverence, I was decent to all even
if in solitary many times I have cried.
Let me wrap up the game; the game that we both have
played together.

32. Arguments

Do I need to pick up this argument with you anymore
for I am afraid if I can even suitably blame you,
as I know I am also equally involved in your every sin?
Your innocent face sinks in my heart like the sun that
disappears at far.
You had once felt the ripples of love in your heart
Was it for me? Tell me cunningly if you are shy of the
truth
Hadn't we agreed to walk together till that next corner
Till our Sun sets and we become a part of that darkness
Answer me once, if you have a heart; a heart that still
beats.

33. The holy drunkard

I am a drunkard, the unknown of the world surrounds
me,
Intoxicated, I roam around the open roads that end
inside me.
I make my drink and pour it over my heart
Like an ardent devotee pours holy water over the idol of
the mighty lord.
Celebrations are unchanging, and sorrows pass in a jiffy,
Between the wee hours and the end of the day, I remain
engrossed in me.
My wears are old and torn as my crumbling body
Neither do I fit to the likings of the moral advocates of
this society.
I remain high and tipsy as I sip the Potion of your divine
affection
In my heart, I have placed my God and his highest
temple.

34. The aching heart

She poured her heart's age-old agony into my heart
like a bar lady pours ageing wine into a sparkling new
wine glass.
I looked at its colour, smelled it and swirled it inside my
mouth
before passing it through my throat.
Pain never gets transferred from mouth to mouth
but probably when you hold her hand in your hand.
Today, keep my glass filled to the brim, O Enchanter!
I will drink till morning and till I empty your every
decanter.

35. The final call

Who is she, knocking at my door at this hour of the day
When the king of the day has abdicated the throne and
the moon has conspired for it.
I am yet to kindle the lamp in front of my lord.
I am in two minds, whether to open the shackles of the
door for her
Or like a wanton wind let her pass by.
Something mysterious is hanging in the air that is
beyond my understanding.
The colours fail to give it character and it has an
outlandish feeling
The gongs of faraway temple bell are yet to soothe my
quivering self.
Am afraid that sooner or later she will hold my skinny
hands
And take me far away through that unknown fountain of
bright fairy lights.
I know not whether that shall be eternal or a mere part
of my absolute destination.

36. Soul

Did you know, many times I have tried to dive deep into
your eyes
through that white submarine that floats in the middle in
a partial disguise.
Like an adept sea-diver, I have passed the long shaft
that joins your eyes with the extreme corner of your
heart.
I searched for traces of contentment, trust and maybe
some preserved petals of hope.
Alas, I can collect some strewn flowers of marigolds
separated from garland offered to lords.
In the base of your heart, I saw that hopeful solitary
boatman waiting for ages for the slack waters,
He has to sail nautical miles unaccompanied; spending
several dawns and dusks before touching the shores.
Also found a letter, half written and scratched; fearful of
misunderstanding; away from deceits.
And a discarded amputated doll, sobbing at
merrymaking days spent in ancient.
At final, when I entered the middle of the heart, it was

light, more light, eye-filling light
that envisaged untouched, pure and indomitable soul of
some primaeval might.

37. Loneliness

For long and quiet hours, I sit looking at the river that
turns oppositely, caressing my feet.
The waned rocks that play hide and seek among the
heaps of white sand
got receded from water in nature's dismay.
The emptiness of my heart grows like a spine
that has grown in me with the passing days.
Catching age, receding hairline,
I got entangled in more earthy sways.
Friends I had, friends they claim,
don't know who stays.
At that straight horizon,
the sun that has to drown today
shall set free several ghosts; scary and unknown
that dance over the corpses of my deeds of olden days

38. My slumber

I was in a delusion when I woke up from my untimely,
undesirable nap at dusk.
When I saw outside my window with my half-opened
eyes, I couldn't fathom a lot.
Have I lost my control over the cycle of fast withdrawing
day and unhurried expanding dark?
Holding my head between my hands, I sat unmoved as if
I were an unyielding piece of deadlog.
I got scared when far away, the Sun had gone downhill
leaving me with haunting dark and indomitable shock.
I remorse, I would have the supremacy to hold the
disappearance of the Sun, had I not slept ill-timed,
I could have kept it alive in my life if I stayed awake like
a steady rock.
Now Moon shines at a far distance on that
unapproachable horizon,
Huh, only a mere reflection of my own Sun.
I know, in this play, I lost to a pal and equally to no one.

39. Cobweb

It happens that I tend to feed and caress my thinking
horses.
O, I prefer to look at the world and its colour using my
limited senses,
Afraid of getting deceived and trampled; created a partial
shroud out of fear.
Never placed a hint of adoration in front of my well-
wishers; Even though I know they are so dear.
My miserable mind unknowingly stitches web for
fencing the likely scoundrels,
I find it difficult now to look straight into their eyes as if
am mid of some hapless mourners.
It clogs my heart and chokes my voice and I long to get a
fresh source of air,
I was afraid as I got entangled in the cobweb stitched by
my mind out of some strange fear.

40. The quicksand

My expectations ran before my truth and lingered in the
absence of evidence.
Time and again, I find my feelings innocently striding in
some tempting quicksand.
And my efforts to come out of it only allow my heart to
sink to its extreme end.
If I have a heart of gold, then why does it tend to break
as if a glassful of water slips from my hand?
My sleeps are meagre and are punctured with a feeling
of dejectedness
My expectations are outnumbered but glint profound
genuineness
O Traveller of inner and barren roads of my heart, accept
my humble request
Don't curse the paucity of my granary before the end of
the harvest.

41. Open sky

Thy vast open sky as if long stretched hands of my
charmer
Enticing me to embrace and accept her unconditionally
and forever.
Your eyes speak everything that your lips desist to,
I had resisted the physical me but I couldn't what the
heart was up to.
Long ago have left 'I' for the selfless and fulfilling 'We'
As if my vanity got enrobed in frugal and simple living.
If I look at the sky again, what not it has accommodated
in its altering hues
Lots of simmering assurance and invincible pain I have
put in to be with you.

42. Longing

Your divinity I have understood when I longed so
impatiently for you,
As if everything has happened that day,
The better part of my age has passed and all is yet new.
I had spent my days finding ways to come near to you.
Nights had schemed scandalously for our separation,
When my eyes' cups were filled with my life full of you,

Seeds that were sown in our childhood have grown and
flowered
The barren space of my heart has waited several seasons
for you, shine or shower
Alas, now no more I can shield it from the wanton storm
to get it uprooted
And I know now, in this life even the sight of your
untouched shadow is not fated.

43. Love

I immersed my soul into that perennial flow of deep
fathomless streams
My long-held shame, misery and melancholy have
washed away; making me immaculate and clean.
I have lent my ears to birds of Springtime and have
heard the babble of newly born breeds,
I have dipped the stem of roses in elixir, to colour my
lover's eyelids.
Today am short of words to write an ode on my mate's
fine-looking eyebrows
But I have kept the doors of my heart ajar to exchange
my love in lieu of your sorrows
The love of July rains attracts the blackest of the clouds
over the thirsty land
The pitter-patter echoes the contentment and love of
every life around.

44. Death

Shall fly like a high hovering Eagle that disappears on a
faraway horizon.
The horizon where his sky meets my earth,
The horizon where both the petals of my lips shall meet
to remain forever quiet,
The horizon where the eyelids of my inquisitive eyes
shall meet to remain forever blind.
No sudden fatal blow, no jet of blood will spout out my
veins,
Maybe I shall be in my deep slumber; fortunate if I have
no pain.
Alas, the grains of sand shall slip from the fist, whatever
I do.
Attar has to be with the wind, even if I try to hold it with
a corkscrew.

45. It ends here

It will end and gradually disappear,
like the incense stick burns in utter silence,
while the doors are kept ajar.
The journey of a thousand thoughts,
the promise of a sun and moon,
a love ballad,
happy hours' blithely croon
togetherness to sustain.
You and me, the promise of a kiss and caress
and love and care, selfless
all will cease to happen
once your river merges with another ocean.
Am afraid; my dinghy is small; will not be able to
weather
the slaps of massive brackish waves.
The ocean is vast, for I don't dare to cross;
alone and far.